Manatees

Gentle Sea Cows

Dr. Richard A. NeSmith

Love of Nature Series

ISSUE 15

Applied **P**rinciples of **E**ducation & Learning

APE-Learning

© 2020 Richard A. NeSmith
Love of Nature Series

All Rights Reserved.

No part of this book may be reproduced, transmitted, or stored in any form or by any means except for your own personal use without the author's express, written permission. All graphs, drawings, and charts are created by the author or utilize public illustrations according to fair use for teaching, research, scholarship, and reporting. Some photos are those of the authors, and some are creative commons licensed. Special thanks to the following who contributed pro-bono from their collections.[i] Thank you all.

This book contains material used under the "Fair Use" of copyrighted material as provided for in section 107 of the U.S. Copyright Law. Every attempt has been made to provide credit to outside organizations or individuals who have provided images, illustrations, documents, or other information.

dr.nesmith@gmail.com

http://richardnesmith.obior.cc

All images in this book are copyright by their respective photographers.

Dr. Richard A. NeSmith
Winter Haven, FL 33884

Dec 2020

ISBN: 9798694494922

FLESCH-KINCAID GRADE LEVEL: 8.4

Manatees
(Order: Sirenia, Family: Trichechus)

Manatees are funny, egg-shaped, warm-blooded mammals with thick leathery skin that spend their entire lives in the water—most of that time in the gulf or ocean. Genetically, they are most closely related to elephants and are essential aquatic *pachyderms*. As the sea cools during the winter months, manatees move inland to springs where warmer water maintains a constant temperature of 72°F (22.2°C).

Manatees are from the Order Sirenia. They have a history recorded from Roman mythology. The *sirens* were make-believe creatures thought to be dangerous. They were nearly always depicted as females, half-human, and half sea creatures. The Sirens are said to lure nearby sailors with their beautiful singing voices and enchanting music to shipwreck on their island's rocky coast.

Virgil and Ovid, two Roman poets, suggested these sirens lived along a chain of small islands called Sirenum scopuli. Here, the funny notion is that the manatees are the gentlest of all the animals in nature and certainly not dangerous creatures. It is believed that scurvy-ridden sailors near death from dehydration envisioned seeing females in the sea with fishtails, which they referred to as mermaids. Possibly what the sailors were hallucinating were the manatees.

Christopher Columbus recorded such an event on his journey to discover the New World. While in the Caribbean, he recorded in his logbook in 1493 his sighting of a *mermaid*. He mentioned that the mermaid was not as beautiful as sailors had been led to believe.

The total population of all manatees in the world has been estimated by scientists to be approaching 15,000. That is a very small number, but manatees were removed from the

1967 *endangered species* classification to *threatened* species status in 2017.[1] Close attention needs to remain on these mammals due to their small population. Many scientists predict that these endangered animals will likely become extinct if they are not closely protected.[2]

There are three species[3] of manatee, distinguished primarily by where they live. There are the West Indian manatee, the Amazonian manatee, and the African manatee. All of these spend most of their lives in the saltwater oceans. However,

---

[1] Reports stated that in the 1960s there were a few hundred manatees present. Present count is estimated 6,000 today. The total reported above includes all three species of manatees. Removal from the *endangered species* list is a questionable move for an animal with such a small population and gene pool.

[2] The following insert is a quote from *Conservation Biology*, 1997. "A 10% increase in adult mortality would drive the population to extinction over a 1000-year time scale, whereas a 10% decrease in adult mortality would allow slow population growth. A 10% decrease in reproduction would also result in extinction. We conclude that management must focus on retaining and improving the conditions under which manatee demography operates." Marmontel, Miriam & Humphrey, Stephen & O'Shea, Thomas. (1997). Population Viability Analysis of the Florida Manatee (Trichechus manatus latirostris), 1976–1991. Conservation Biology. 11. 10.1046/j.1523-1739.1997.96019.x.

[3] A fourth species is still awaiting scientific confirmation.

they all seek freshwater streams during cold seasons and for drinking. **_Manatees do not drink salt water_** but can go for one to two weeks before needing to locate freshwater sources for consumption. The focus in this issue is on the West Indian manatee. It ranges along the North American east coast from Florida to Brazil.

Most aquatic animals are either able to live in fresh or saltwater. A few, like the manatee, have adapted to both. This flexibility requires a unique physiological mechanism to handle dehydration or water buildup. Manatee's kidneys counter these issues by filtering blood to control salt levels and maintain water balance. The urinary bladder stores urine until it is advantageous to dump it into the environment.

The name "manatee" is a word from pre-Columbian Taíno

MANATEES: GENTLE SEA COWS

people. It merely means "breast." Some like to refer to this as the Florida manatee, but that is more of a wishful moniker. But we will inevitably use the reference "Florida manatee" endearingly, but doing so knowing it is merely a local name. The scientific name of the West Indian manatee is Trichechus *manatus latirostris*. Manatus is the **species** name, and there are two other **subspecies**. Thus the subspecies name for our so-called *Florida* manatee favorite is *latirostris*. Because of their diet of seagrasses and other aquatic plants, manatees are also nicknamed **sea cows**. The Indo-Pacific cousins of the manatees are called

dugongs. Dugongs, however, with their dolphin fluke-like tail, are strictly marine mammals.

Range

Though residents of the United States southeastern

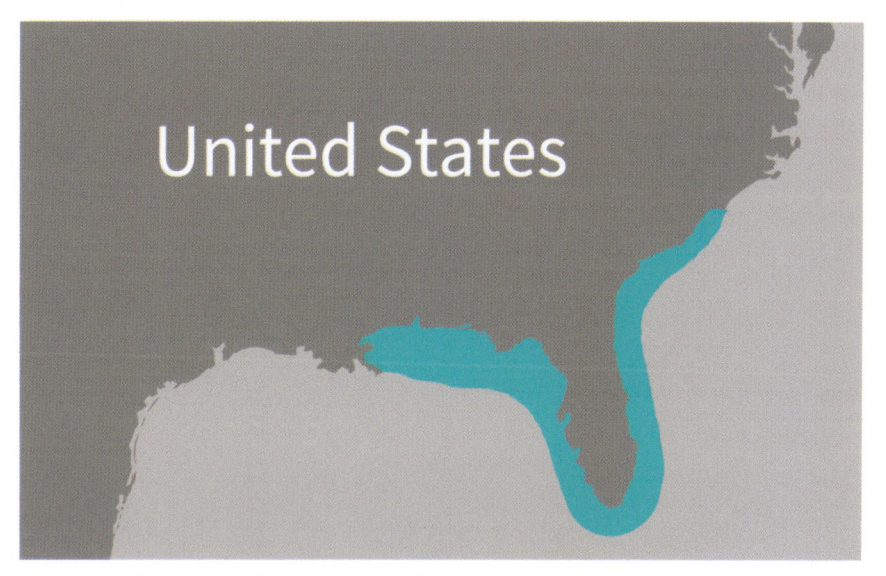

Distribution of the West Indian manatee population. *Courtesy of Marine Mammal Commission. https://www.mmc.gov/wp-content/uploads/Florida-Manatee-R2.png*

coastlines, most manatees tend to spend the summer months in the Gulf of Mexico. However, some "vacation" or migrate along the Georgia/South Carolina coasts, up as far north as Cape Cod, Massachusetts, and as far *south* as Cuba's north shore. And they are traveling as far *west* as Louisiana. However, a few have been spotted vacationing along the Texas coastline down to Mexico.

Characteristics

The West Indian manatee is a huge, gray aquatic mammal with a body that tapers to a flat, paddle-shaped tail. An adult will average 900 lbs. (408 kg) and be 10 feet long. Females tend to be larger and heavier (sexual dimorphism). The largest manatees found grew to 15 ft. (4.6 meters) and weighed 3,913 lbs. (1,775 kilograms). At birth, a baby (calf) can weigh about 30 kilograms (66 lbs.).

They have two forelimbs, called flippers, with three to four toenails on each fin. They have a wrinkled head and face with whiskers on the snout. They tend to swim in slow motion and do so like that of a dolphin. They can swim up to 20-30 miles per hour during distress, but only in short bursts. Their swimming speed averages three to five miles an hour.

Since manatees are mammals, they have lungs and breathe air. This means they may spend most of their time underwater, but they must surface to breathe. The nostrils on a manatee are on the top of the nose and act like a whale's blowhole. As they come to the surface, generally, their back arches up, and the back or the head breaks the surface before their nostrils do. As an aside, they are growing an entire biome on their backs.

Manatees exhale (*expiration*) forcefully upon reaching the water's surface. They then inhale (*inspiration*) fresh air. After 3 or 5 repeated breaths and the manatee is ready to descend again slowly. You and I have two lungs like the manatees, but ours works as a single unit. The manatees' lungs are super-charged. First, they can use their rib cage muscles to compress their lung volume and make their bodies denser. Secondly, they have a diaphragm that divides the animal in half across the chest: a *hemi*diaphragm (*hemi-* meaning half). That is like having two diaphragms running the length of most of their torso. Thirdly, manatees have bronchial muscles, which strengthen the muscular diaphragm. They inhale and exhale better than nearly any other mammal. Each lung can exchange air *separately*.

This modified respiratory system helps facilitate rapid air exchange and ensure carbon dioxide (CO_2) is fully exhaled. Then a large amount of air containing oxygen (O_2) is inhaled. Because of this extensive air exchange, manatees take in more oxygen with each breath. A manatee can typically hold its breath for 20 minutes underwater. However, most of the time, it will float to the top for a breath of air every 4 or 5 minutes. Not a long time in comparison to seals and dolphins.

The lengthy manatee lungs also help them rise and fall (float) in the water and spread out the buoyancy along the body's length. So, the lungs also act as their "BC,"

buoyancy compensator, a flotation device. This buoyancy effect is used by them rather than to swim up or down actively. While sleeping, the rib cage muscles relax, causing the lung volume to expand their lung volume and carry them towards the surface. They grab a fresh breath and effortlessly sink back underwater.

Buoyancy becomes an essential factor when considering that the manatee's ribs and other long bones lack marrow cavities, producing a very **dense** and relatively *heavy* skeleton.[4]

Manatees are peaceful, but they are quite vocal. They possess a larynx and can make squeals, squeaks, whistles, chirps, clicking noises, as well as the sounds of air blowing as they exhale at the surface. Their hearing is very good,

---

[4] Bone marrow is where most mammal's bodies create red blood cells. In manatees, this seems to be restricted to the *centra* of the vertebrae and sternum.

and they may have the ability to hear low-frequency sounds. Mammals, as do the manatees, possess hair on their bodies (especially on their nose). These act to help detect minimal movement in the water.

Though small eyes, manatees' eyes are well-developed. Eyesight in the water is very good and can detect objects from quite far. They possess rods and cones, indicating they can probably see color, as well as dim and bright light. The small eyes have **nictitating membranes** drawn over them for protection underwater but not preventing or distracting vision. Manatees do not have outer eyelids or eyelashes. Unlike humans, their eye muscles close in a circular motion, like an aperture on a camera.

Diet

Manatees are, generally speaking, vegetarians (herbivores). However, some have been observed feeding on clams and fish. They feed almost exclusively on plants that grow in fresh and saltwater environments. Freshwater plants include pickerelweed, water lettuce, alligator weed, water celery, eelgrass, coontail, musk grass, and exotic species like water hyacinth and hydrilla.

They also eat saltwater plants, such as seagrasses, manatee grass, shoal grass, turtle grass, sea clover, widgeon grass, and marine algae. Manatees can often be seen nosing onto the edge of a shoreline munching on tender plants and grasses. They love human-grown lettuce and greens, but keep in mind there may be laws preventing one from feeding manatees. A rule of thumb is that it is not a good

Manatee grass is not actually grass at all. It looks a lot like spaghetti in clumps in the Gulf of Mexico.. It is a member of the monocot Manateegrass family, the Cymodoceaceae. Genus: Species: Syringodium filiforme.

practice to feed wild animals, but granted, though there are exceptions.

Manatees spend 6 to 8 hours a day eating. They graze by crawling up on the bottom on their flippers. On average, manatees feast on 100-200 pounds of soggy, sandy seagrasses and weeds every day. A manatee consumes food equal to 10%-15% of its body weight. Their molar (back grinding) teeth grow their whole lives, but the tiny sand granules on their food gradually wear down their teeth. Like lots of mammals, eventually, their teeth fall out. They are disposable. Also, they do not have front teeth to rip and tear food off, as we do.

The ever-growing molars push teeth forward, replacing those that have fallen out. So, you probably will not see a snaggletooth manatee. Behind the lips are roughed, complex ridges that are used to grasp food with the lower jaw. Upon tearing the food, it is guided to the molars for grinding.

Because manatees do not have front incisors to rip or tear plants to be eaten, they have an upper **prehensile** lip (much like an elephant's trunk) that is split, producing the left and right sides. Prehensile means they can use it to grip on to an object, much like a monkey's tail can grab onto a limb. In essence, they can hold a batch of Romaine lettuce while chewing other food simultaneously. Only, it's vegetation the manatees are pulling at and manipulating. The lips have seven different muscles in which they can use to tear at plants. But, flexible and muscular flippers aid in guiding food into the manatee's mouth. The molars are of different types and shapes and seem to provide ample grinding of plant matter. Sandpapery seagrasses wear down

the weak enameled teeth, which continually grow through

the manatee's life. Front molars are shed while back molars wear down (about 0.0394 inches, or only one millimeter per month; *less than the width of a penny*) and are replaced.

Having teeth like a cow, manatees cannot truly defend themselves or hurt a person by biting. Their teeth are back far in the mouth, and one biologist has noted one can put their entire hand inside a manatee's mouth before you would even reach the teeth. By now, you can see why manatees are nicknamed *sea cows*.

Though manatees feed in the water, they manage to remove most of the water before swallowing their food. Their stomach contents enter relatively dry. This *bolus* of food is well mixed with digestive enzymes from their large salivary glands, which lubricate and begin the initial digestion of carbohydrates.

Mammals cannot break down the main product in plants, called **cellulose**. But bacteria can. This dilemma means that the manatees must have a means of doing this. A manatee's digestive system then is much like that of a horse. Manatees have **hind-gut digesters** as opposed to fore-gut digesters (like the cow). So, more of the digestive processes occur further along in the intestinal tract. This form of digestion requires *time* for the bacteria to break down chemical bonds through ***fermentation***. When this happens, energy is released to be used by the cells. It takes about seven days for material to pass through the manatee's digestive system.

Habitat

The Western Indian Manatees are shallow-water mammals since they must feed off the bottom or onshore edges. They inhabit rivers, bays, canals, estuaries (tidal mouth of a large river), and coastal areas. They move freely between fresh, saline, and brackish water. It becomes clear that their range is directly linked to their habitat needs. As winter approaches and temperatures drop, manatees are greatly affected by

colder waters. It is natural for manatees in cool water to lose body heat faster than producing it due to their low body fat percentage. This results in **hypothermia**.

Manatees, therefore, cannot tolerate long periods exposed to frigid water (below 68° F). Cold water drains the body heat *25 times more quickly* than cold air. This low temperature can cause ***shock,*** which then causes an immediate loss of breathing control. As the Gulf of Mexico and the Atlantic Ocean falls below 70°F (21°C) during the winter months, manatees are motivated to move into warm water refuge areas.

This need for warmer waters explains why the Florida

manatee seeks inlet streams, springs, rivers, and even lakes along rivers and waterways. They need to avoid the drop in temperature during winter months. Manatees need warm water to survive, and the 72°F temperature of the springs tends to be constant.[5] Since the food source is quite adequate in these warmer waters, some manatees remain year-round.

Behavior

Manatees are nonaggressive and non-territorial. Though manatees were once thought to be solitary animals, they

---

[5] Spring temperatures, however, do actually fluctuate some (66 to 97 °F). Cooler water temperatures can result from water upwelling from deeper in the aquifer. Or, warmer waters can result from deep water closer to hot vents or underwater hotspots, such as volcano activity (not in Florida, of course).

seem to do quite a bit of social interaction with others. They appear to have periods of being semi-sociable (in pairs or small groups). Manatees have been observed participating in what appeared to be semi-organized playful activities, such as bodysurfing and follow-the-leader.

During such events, they will synchronize their actions, such as breathing, changing directions, and diving with one another. And, at times, they nuzzle one another and vocalize while playing. When not feeding, they are resting, and that can amount from two to twelve hours per day. The rest of the time is spent traveling, curiously investigating things that catch their attention, or interacting and socializing with other manatees. They often enjoy checking out humans as well.

Manatees are very curious creatures. Despite having one of the smallest mammalian brains, they are quite intelligent. Their brains are physically very smooth, having few of the surface 'folds' associated with higher intelligence in other mammals.[6]

Scientists have found them adaptive to tasks and problem-

---

[6] The human brain, in comparision, is very convoluted (possesses many folds and wrinkles).

solving as well as dolphins (one of the smartest animals on the planet). They often approach swimmers out of curiosity and seem to enjoy the encounters. However, just like people, they usually have their socializing limits and will display some avoidance behaviors. When that occurs, let them be. Respect that you are in their home. Also, keep in mind that manatees are a protected species. It is illegal to "annoy, molest, harass, or disturb any manatee" in the wild. The best rule of thumb is "do not touch" but rather to *let them do the approach and initiate contact*. And, as cute as they are, do not feed them.

Though they are really defenseless, even alligators give manatees the right of way. One biologist reported that when a manatee enters a river and wants to pass through, it will swim up to alligators obstructing its path and bump or nudge them to move.[7] When it comes to curiosity, manatees

---

[7] Patrick Rose, an aquatic biologist and executive director of the Save the Manatee Club.

have no apparent fear of approaching alligators, especially

if they are in the way. Touching them, nudging them, and even pushing them out of the way is not uncommon.

Partly, the manatee's size gives them the advantage. Alligators do not seem to see them as prey. Gentle respect appears to be the rule.

Swimming for the manatees is a matter of the body waving up and down. A swimming manatee might be compared to a sheet on a clothesline *waving* in the wind. The manatee swims with up and down (dorsoventrally) motions of its body and fluke. This method or motion of swimming is similar to that of dolphins and whales.

Reproduction

Manatees are not monogamous, meaning they do not pair off for life as some animal species. Mating season begins in the spring and goes to early summer.[8] A single female, or cow, will be followed by a group of a dozen or more males or bulls, forming a *mating herd* during breeding. The reproductive rate for manatees is low. The age of sexual maturity for females and males is about five years. On average, one calf is born every two to five years, and twins

---

[8] Although breeding and birth may occur at any time during the year, there appears to be a broad spring-summer calving peak.

are extremely rare.

The gestation (pregnancy) period for the West Indian Manatee is approximately 13 months, and generally, only a single calf is born. Bulls have little interaction with the cow or calf and assume no responsibility in raising the calf.

The calf is born underwater and can swim to the surface independently. It can also vocalize at, or soon after, birth. Like dolphins, the cow may nudge the calf towards the surface if necessary. The cow's teats (udders) are located behind the mom's flippers and frequently visited by the calf for nursing. Within a few weeks, the calf can forage with its mother and eat plants. The cows are often seen with their calves. The calf can be dependent upon its mothers for up to two years.

Miscellaneous

Manatees have a ***symbiotic*** relationship with other organisms, such as fish. This type of symbiotic relationship is called ***mutualism***, for both organisms benefit from the other. Small fish are permitted to stay around and eat at the algae, barnacles, parasites, and dead skin on the manatee's backs. The fish benefit from the food provided, while the manatees benefit by being rid of unneeded and sometimes parasitic organisms.

Manatees are not known to harm anything. They spend their days grazing on seagrasses and freshwater vegetation. Though slow, massive, and passive, manatees have no natural predators or enemies. Sharks would attack them; however, they seldom share the same environment. Manatees are more shallow-water animals, whereas the sharks tend to be more in line with deep-sea fishing. There are seasons when tiger sharks and bull sharks troll more shallow waters and occasionally attack a weak or young manatee. Or, they may strike a manatee stuck in the mud, alone, or injured. The notion of being injured is important as shark behavior becomes frenzied if an animal appears injured or is losing blood. Most sharks, however, hunt much smaller prey. They are just too small to go after such a large animal.

Alligators, as mentioned, have no interest in preying on manatees. About the only real predator or danger to manatees are humans, and more particularly, humans' motorboats. Watercraft collisions/boat strikes (60 % cause of implicated deaths) and boat propellers (40% cause of death) slice through manatees' skin. Disease and cold also take a toll. Nearly every manatee has experienced with boat propellers, for they have the scars to prove it. Such injuries or fatalities happen so frequently that the Florida Fish and Wildlife Conservation Commission has a designated phone line for reporting dead manatees. Manatees have continued to thrive since being protected. However, their populations are minimal compared to most animals. Issues such as inbreeding can become issues causing abnormalities, still-births, and even being wiped out by virus- or bacteria-

Dugong cousin, getting a remora "car wash" and removal of algae, barnacles, and parasites.

inflicting diseases. One study found that any West Indies manatee is a cousin to the next. This factor will continue to be monitored, but small gene pools have caused some animals to become extinct. Unfortunately, that seems to be the prognosis made by many scientists for the manatee. At present, manatees can live to be 40-60 years old.

Boaters need to follow the rules and the laws established in designated "No Wake" zones.[9] Your boat traveling at high speeds can strike a manatee and kill it or knock it unconscious. An unconscious manatee drowns. Prop injuries can be lethal or can cause such injuries as to become infected, leading to death. Also, and seldom considered by the general public, it is that of slowing down one's boat to avoid unnecessarily destroying significant vegetation and grasses upon which the manatee must have to survive.

Lyngbya is a large-celled, filamentous, mat-forming cyanobacterium (blue-green alga). It occurs in freshwater and especially flourishes in Florida's spring-fed waters. Courtesy of the Florida Department of Environmental Protection

---

[9] Currently, 18 Florida counties have manatee protection zones.

Degrading the habitat also threatens manatees' survival rate, whether it is caused by blocking natural springs or building up the coastline for residential or commercial use. One example was the intentional removal of eelgrass. Upon doing so, the invasive blue-green algae called **Lyngbya** took over in many of the rivers.[10] It is a slimy filament that now fills much of the rivers. It chokes out the sunlight and reduces the water's oxygen concentration. Periodic fish kills occur, or fish simply fail to return to the river. It not only depletes water-oxygen concentrations, but its slimy filaments also *prevent* the native grasses from returning.

Some environmental conservation groups are beginning to make an impact. But at this rate, it may be too little too late.

---

[10] *Lyngbya is a real threat to most streams.* "It uses several mechanisms to ensure it stays happy and healthy. Its thick glycoprotein sheath adds an extra physical barrier that fortifies the cell wall. On top of this layer is an established microbial community, or microbiota, that works mutualistically with the Lyngbya. The microbiota defends its host by helping to gather resources for growth or shielding it from environmental and chemical impacts (i.e. algaecides)." (Naturelake Biosciences, (n.d.) Available at: https://naturalake.com/beating-lyngbya/

More people need to get concerned and ask for more to be done to protect these manatee's habitats. Protecting these sanctuaries protects all the organisms that call it home. Some restoration is taking place in which decades of death and decay are being removed from once pristine springs and rivers. Dead material can accumulate several feet deep. Some natural spring vents have closed or become plugged up from sludge.

Residential and commercial use of fertilizers (phosphorous) run off or seep back into the water table. These introduced chemicals cause the blooming of **bacteria** and **fungi** and even feeds the growth of **red tides** in bays or open waters. Poisoned water creating such blooms choke the sunlight and oxygen from the water, causing fish kills. What was a healthy spring environment becomes a lifeless wasteland.

As this occurs, manatees will be forced to avoid their warmer-water homes or die from the contamination.

Taking care of the environment requires taking care of the water. Taking care of the water then provides the manatees with a chance of survival. Though the manatees are presently off of the endangered list, it would appear that some of the springs might already occupy that status. In the past few years, a record number of manatees have died from unknown causes. Not everyone wants to admit that we might be poisoning the springs, and in doing so, poisoning the manatees and all that live within the once paradise environments.

MANATEES: GENTLE SEA COWS

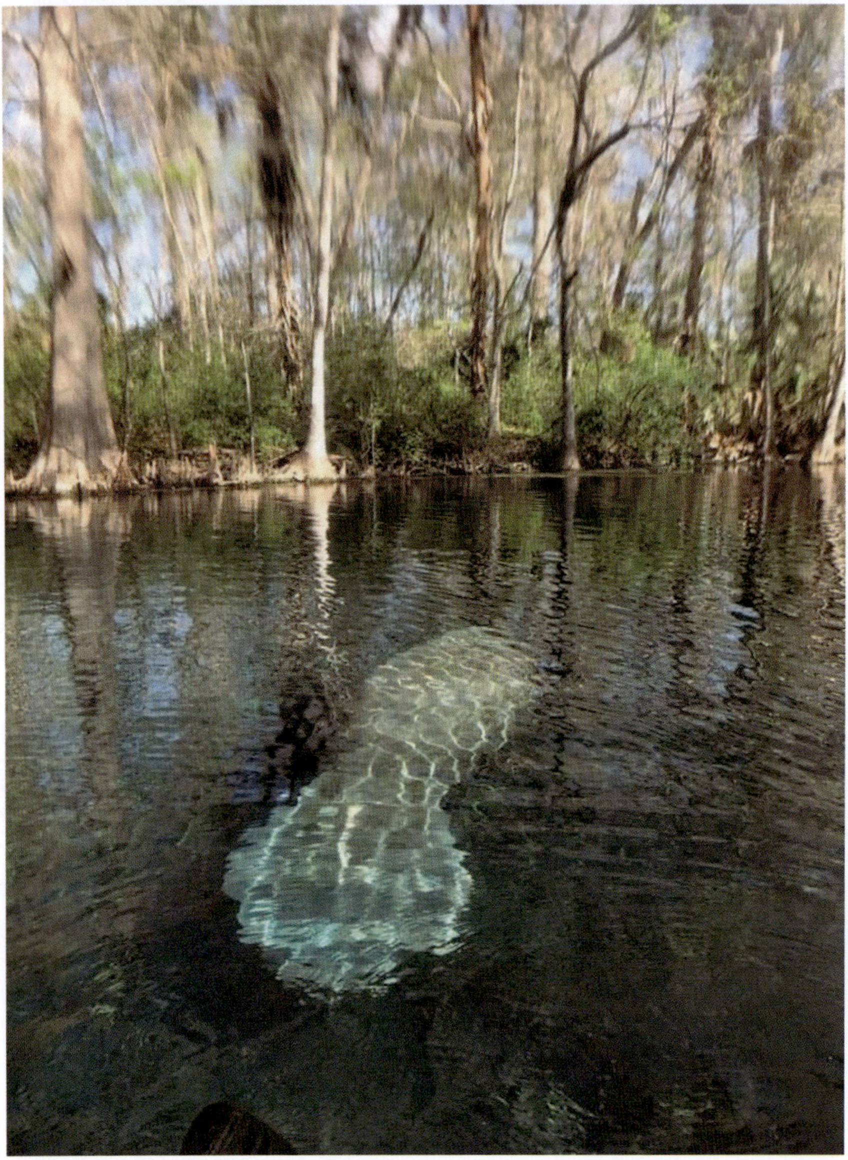

REVIEW

1. What are the three types of manatees in the world?

2. What is the correct name for the Florida manatee?

3. What is the genus, species, and subspecies name for the manatee focused on in this book?

4. What seems to be the greatest biological danger to manatees?

5. What seems to be the greatest human danger to manatees?

6. What happened when people removed the eelgrass in most Florida springs and rivers?

7. What two things seem to motivate the West Indian Manatee to enter the Florida springs?

8. How does a manatee move up and down in the water?

9. What is hypothermia, and how does it occur in manatees?

10. How long can a manatee hold its breath underwater?

MANATEES: GENTLE SEA COWS

40

MANATEES: GENTLE SEA COWS

MANATEE AND HER BABY

COLORING PAGE

http://www.supercoloring.com/coloring-pages/manatee-mother-and-baby

Manatees: Gentle Sea Cows

Name:_____

Carefully read the statement or clue. Record the coerrect letters in the spaces provided. Use the Word Bank, if necessary.

Word Bank: grazing | prehensile | alligators | five | temperature | manatees | Sirens | boat | digesters | dugong | threatened | hypothermia | population | symbiotic | Floridia

Across
3. Name for relationships such as manatees allowing fish to pick flora and fauna off of their backs?
8. Though off of the endangered species list at this time, manatees are on the _____ species list.
9. 15,000 represents the _____ of the West Indian Manatees.
10. Greek mythology may have linked to the _____.
13. The greatest danger to manatees are _____ strikes.
14. Body loses heat faster than it can produce it.
15. Like a horse, manatees are hind-gut _____.

Down
1. Even large _____ do not seem to attack manatees.
2. The 'common' name for the West Indian Manatee is the _____ Manatee.
4. Manatees spend most of their day _____.
5. Cousin of the manatee?
6. The Florida springs tend to stay at 72oF water _____.
7. Mature female manatees give birth to one calf about every one calf is born every two to _____ years
11. The manatee's lips are funny-looking because they are _____.
12. Columbus and other sailors thought they had seen mermaids but they probably witnessed _____.

42

MANATEES: GENTLE SEA COWS

INTERESTING SOURCES TO CONSIDER

8 things you didn't know about manatees. PBS News Hour. Available at: https://www.pbs.org/newshour/science/8-things-didnt-know-manatees#:~:text=1.,up%20in%20Cape%20Cod%20waters

All About Manatees for Children: Manatee Video for Kids. FreeSchool. Available at: https://youtu.be/ruSqRvCxi-s

Blue Spring Florida Manatees State Park. Florida TV. Available at: https://youtu.be/BwON-wG7Puc

Can We Save The Manatee? (Wildlife Documentary: The Blue Realm | Real Wild. Available at: https://youtu.be/wrREWMgYNQk

Crystal Manatees - Florida Manatee Wildlife. Available at: https://youtu.be/_AvjXSEWBXk

From Mermaids to Manatees: the Myth and the Reality. Available at: https://ocean.si.edu/ocean-life/marine-mammals/mermaids-manatees-myth-and-reality

Guy Keeps Saving Baby Manatees. The Dodo Heroes. Available at: https://youtu.be/exyhpLue3SI

Manatees Are the "Sea Cows" of the Coasts. National Geographic Wild. Available at: https://youtu.be/DlJy7HQMgSI

Manatees LOVE Video Cameras! Brave Wilderness. Available at: https://youtu.be/hNT83a7Bl1c

Manatees: Conserving a Marine Mammal. ChangingSeatsTV. Available from https://youtu.be/U8PT26XwSzk

Meet the Manatees. Nature on PBS. Available at: https://youtu.be/R7-a7UBXT2E

Naturelake Biosciences. (n.d.) Available at: https://naturalake.com/beating-lyngbya/

Ocean Stories 2 - Manatees and Molas. Available at: https://youtu.be/6OQYLyxB8pw

Save the Manatees Web-cams. Available at: https://www.savethemanatee.org/manatees/manatee-webcams/

Underwater Manatee Cam at Blue Spring State Park. Available at: https://youtu.be/771F3a1UTyQ

44

ABOUT THE AUTHOR

Richard NeSmith is a native of Florida, USA. He grew up wading through the swamps of central Florida with his two younger brothers during the pre-Disney era, and unknowingly, falling in love with biology, wildlife, and nature. He has lived in seven American states, twice in Australia, and once in Mexico City. He holds eight university degrees and has taught for 14 years in secondary schools, here and abroad, and another 13 years as a professor in several American universities. His service includes professor of science education, Dean of Education, Campus Dean, as well as an online instructor. His passion for learning (and *how we learn*) did not develop until *after* graduating from high school. His only explanation for this is that *having a goal made all the difference in the world*. He enjoys reading, hiking, nature photography, golf, tennis, and RV camping.

http://richardnesmith.obior.cc

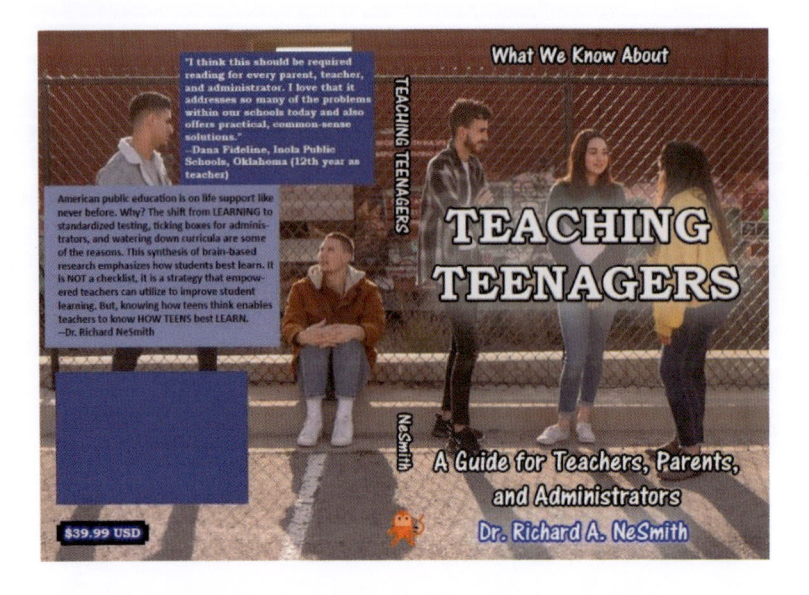

Applied Principles of Education & Learning *presents*

APE-Learning

AMAZON AUTHOR's PAGE:

https://www.amazon.com/author/richardnesmith

Educational, wildlife, and naturalist books Dr. Richard NeSmith.

MANATEES: GENTLE SEA COWS

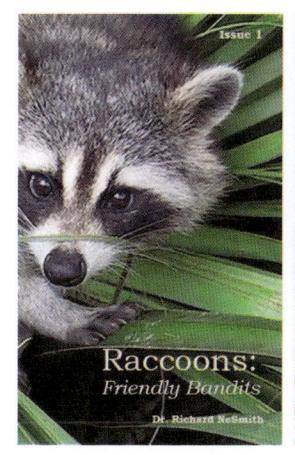

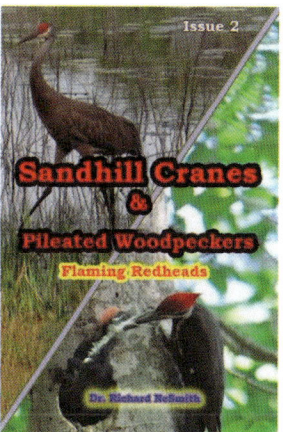

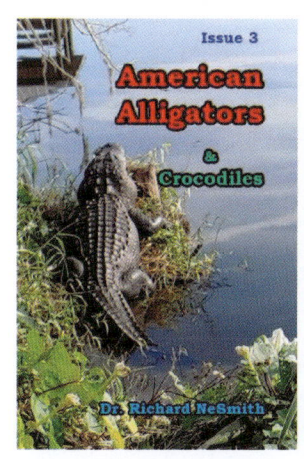

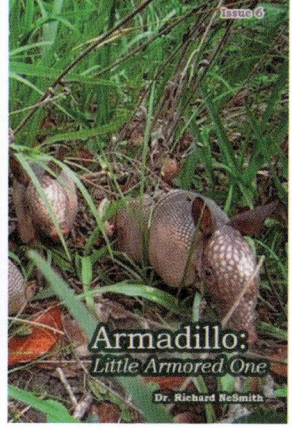

47

MANATEES: GENTLE SEA COWS

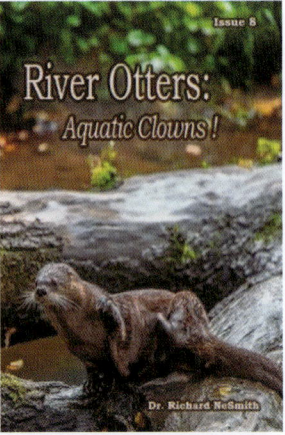

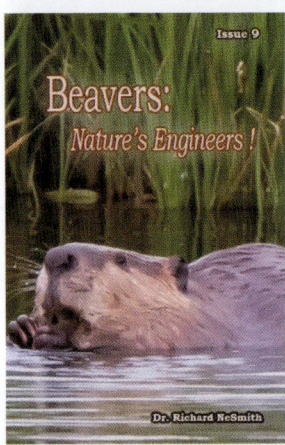

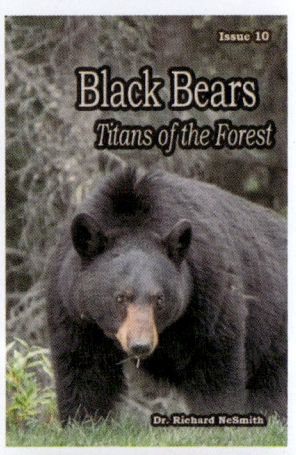

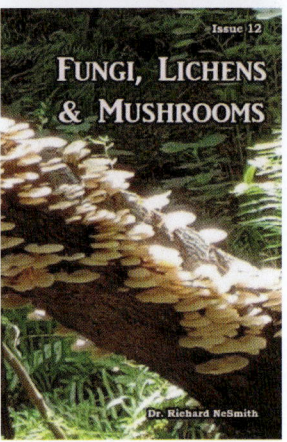

48

Paperbacks: http://amazon.com/author/richardnesmith

e-books: https://bit.ly/3iuCgB3

---

[i] **Special thanks to the following who kindly provided permission to use their photographs.**

From Pixabay: Hans Dietmann, and ASSY.

Special thanks to likeminded friends who love wildlife and who willingly shared their wonderful photos, and many of whom have become my friends: **Alexandrea Deliere, Bette Volland, Cathy Clements, Chelsea Farmer, Dary Dari, Donna Ogden Waring, Dorinda Callander Walker, Dragomir Mijic, Jackie Dibert, Jackie Grill, Jennifer Yost, Jodi Elfenbein Samson, Karen Osbon, Lynette Llagostera, Madeline Vinson, Sara Jones Middlebrook,** and **Stefanie Burlingame.**

And, then there are my special friends and contributors who are always to encouraging and generous in sharing with me their wonderful photos. **Special thanks** to: **Karen Devens, Pam Maniec, Phil Stone, Stacey Diamond, Greg Jowers, DS Damm, Sherri Hardman,** and the *very special*, **Dr. Laurie Aleixo**, who not only contributes but move across the country just to provide medical care to injured and needy manatees.

Thank you to Marine Mammal Commission for the use of their illustration map of the distribution of the West Indian manatee population. https://www.mmc.gov/wp-content/uploads/Florida-Manatee-R2.png. Also special thanks to the **Florida Department of Environmental Protection** for the use of the manatee grass photograph. https://bit.ly/3iJMNaU.

Thank you all.

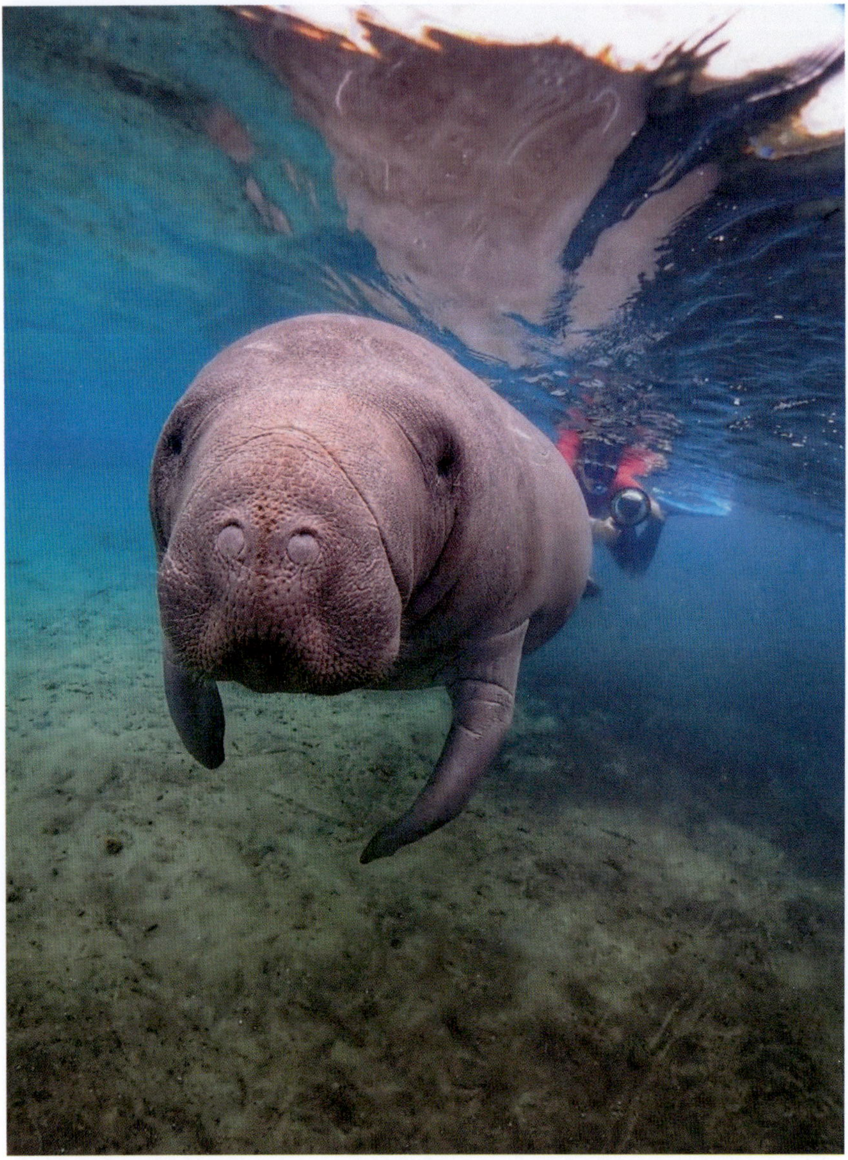